First Ladies' Gowns

Illustrations by Geraldine Lucas

Smithsonian Institution Press
Washington, D.C.

Cover: Ida Saxton McKinley

Consultant for this book: Margaret Brown Klapthor, Curator, Division of Political History, Department of Social and Cultural History, National Museum of American History, Smithsonian Institution

96 95 94 93 92 91   8 7 6 5 4 3

Introduction

One of the most popular exhibits in the entire Smithsonian Institution is the First Ladies Hall in the National Museum of American History, where dresses worn by First Ladies of every presidential administration can be seen in settings based on period White House rooms.

The gowns are displayed on mannequins whose faces are identical, modeled after a classical bust of Cordelia, daughter of Shakespeare's King Lear, by Pierce F. Connelly. The expression of the eyes of each mannequin, the hair styles, the coloring, and the sizes of the figures themselves are different, however, derived from the gowns and based as closely as possible on photographs, paintings, statues, or written descriptions of the individual First Ladies.

The First Lady has not always been the President's wife. At times, for various reasons, a relative or friend has performed the duties of official White House hostess. The rooms the First Ladies occupy in the museum have been decorated, whenever possible, with actual White House or other presidential furniture and accessories to recreate the types of surroundings in which the dresses were worn.

Twenty-nine of the forty-four First Ladies on display in the hall are depicted in this coloring book. They were chosen because their dresses are of particular interest. It should be remembered that the gowns as seen at the Smithsonian have suffered from constant exposure to light and therefore are softer in color than they originally were.

Martha Custis Washington

The *first* First Lady is wearing a dress of salmon-pink faille, its design handpainted in natural colors with native North American wildflowers in the larger medallion spaces and insects in the smaller ones. She holds a brown satin bag. The white lace mob cap she wears was fashionable for social gatherings in the late 18th century.

Abigail Smith Adams   Mrs. Adams wore this dress of brocaded silk, with green and pink decorations on an ivory background, when she was in England while her husband, John Adams, served as the first American minister, 1785–88. The petticoat is quilted pink satin. A white gauze kerchief completes her outfit. The brooch contains locks of her hair, along with hair of her husband and oldest son, who became President John Quincy Adams.

Dolley Payne Madison A contemporary account described this dress, worn by Mrs. Madison to a New Year's Day reception in 1816, as "yellow satin embroidered all over with sprigs of butterflies, not two alike. . . ." Mrs. Madison had exchanged the Quaker caps of her youth for turbans, which she always wore at public functions. This one is pink, reflecting a color in the gown's butterflies.

Louisa Johnson Adams The First lady wears an Empire-style dress with a high waistline and a bell-shaped skirt made of white net festooned with silver braid, worn over a white satin underdress. The white linen handkerchief she holds, measuring a yard square, is of a fine material with dainty embroidery. The harp, which belonged to Mrs. Adams, was in the White House during the John Quincy Adams administration (1825–29).

Emily Tennessee Donelson   This is the earliest inaugural gown in the First Ladies Hall. Mrs. Donelson served as First Lady, until her illness in 1836, for her widower uncle, President Andrew Jackson. Legend has it that the dress—made of gold satin brocaded with a design of rosebuds and violets—was a gift from him. Mrs. Donelson's unusually elaborate hairdo was very fashionable at that time.

Angelica Singleton Van Buren   Mrs. Van Buren acted as First Lady for her widower father-in-law, Martin Van Buren. Her royal blue gown has a hoop skirt—a very popular fashion in the mid-19th century. The heavy skirt, which measures 8 to 10 yards around the hem, is supported by a foundation skirt and a set of hoops. An ostrich plume in the First Lady's dark hair and a forehead jewel complete the regal picture.

Jane Irwin Findlay   Mrs. Findlay, senior White House hostess during the William Henry Harrison administration (1841), wears a dress of dark-brown velvet with leg-of-mutton sleeves. A long-time friend of President and Mrs. Harrison, she came to Washington to assist her foster daughter, Mrs. William Henry Harrison, Jr., who served as First Lady for the one month that her father-in-law was President. The wallpaper is white, with gold stars and a gilt border.

Julia Gardiner Tyler   After his first wife, an invalid, died in the White House, President John Tyler in 1844 married Julia Gardiner, a society belle some 30 years younger than he. Her gown, worn when she was presented at the French court before her marriage, is made of sheer white mull. The bodice and flounces of the skirt are embroidered with silver thread and a pastel flower design.

Sarah Childress Polk   Mrs. Polk wore this gown at the ball honoring the inauguration of her husband, President James K. Polk, in 1845. It is made of blue ribbed silk damask with a poinsettia design. The elaborately carved chair beside the First Lady is of laminated rosewood, similar to furniture used in the White House in the mid-19th century.

Betty Taylor Bliss   Preferring the seclusion of her room, Mrs. Zachary Taylor left the duties of First Lady to her daughter during the brief Taylor administration, 1849–50. President Taylor died after a year and four months in office. "Miss Betty," as she was known, wears a dress of greenish-brown grenadine trimmed with red and brown plaid borders.

Harriet Lane Acting as First Lady during the administration of James Buchanan (1857–61), the only bachelor President, was his attractive young niece. She is shown here wearing her wedding dress, made of white moire taffeta trimmed with white satin and lace. Miss Lane married Henry Elliot Johnston in 1866, a few years after her uncle had retired from public service.

Mary Todd Lincoln   Mrs. Lincoln was especially fond of clothes. Her dress, made of royal purple velvet, has seams piped with white satin; the decorations on bodice and sleeves are of black and white lace. The elaborate candelabrum and the pedestal stand, with its colorful vase of wax flowers, are typical of pieces that might have been found in a White House Victorian parlor of the Civil War era.

Martha Johnson Patterson   Daughter of President Andrew Johnson and the wife of a United States Senator, Mrs. Patterson acted as First Lady in place of her invalid mother. She is represented in the collection by an evening coat, a "bournous," as it was called, made of finely woven cream-colored wool, ornamented with gold braid and tassels. The gold tasseled hood may be worn over the head or pushed back.

Julia Dent Grant   This dress of white and silver brocade was worn by the First Lady to Ulysses S. Grant's second inaugural ball of 1873. The white lace fichu around the shoulders was worn by Mrs. Grant at her husband's first inaugural ball. Fashions at this period were gradually changing from the hoop skirt to the bustle. The draperies here are blue, richly patterned.

Lucretia Rudolph Garfield The First Lady wore this bustle dress at President James A. Garfield's inaugural ball of 1881, which was held in the Smithsonian Institution's Arts and Industries Building. The trimmings of lace, ribbons, and ruchings are of the same satin fabric as the dress. Over the years, the original lavender of the material has faded to a soft gray.

Rose Elizabeth Cleveland Grover Cleveland was a bachelor when he first became President in 1885, so his sister acted as First Lady for a time. Her dress is made of garnet red silk velvet with pink faille at the neckline and skirt inserts. Trimming consists of silver-and-gold braid. The gold chair was used in the Blue Room of the White House; the wallpaper is blue-gray with gold decorations.

Caroline Scott Harrison   For President Benjamin Harrison's inauguration in 1890, his wife wore this dress with a bodice and train made of silver-gray faille; the front skirt panels are of brocade of burr oak design on gray satin. Each panel is edged with apricot silk, veiled with lace. The collar, sleeves, and bodice front are trimmed with silver and gold-bead fringe.

Ida Saxton McKinley The First Lady wore this elegant gown at President William McKinley's second inaugural ball in 1898. It is of heavy white satin, and the front panel of the skirt is embroidered with pearls. Rose-point lace trims bodice, skirt, and sleeves. The high, tight collar was a distinctive fashion note of the time. This was also the era of beautiful fabrics and elaborate styling.

Edith Kermit Carow Roosevelt   This dress of robin's-egg blue brocade, with a design of swallows and pinwheels of gold, was worn by the First Lady at Theodore Roosevelt's inaugural ball of 1905. The material was especially designed and woven for Mrs. Roosevelt in Paterson, New Jersey. The neckline is edged with rose-point lace. Skirts in this period began to fall in an easy, graceful sweep over the hips.

Helen Herron Taft   This white silk chiffon gown was worn by the First Lady at William Howard Taft's inaugural ball of 1909. Designed during a revival of the Empire style, the dress features a high waistline, a train, and a clinging skirt embroidered in silver thread and crystal beads. This was the first dress to be donated by a First Lady to the Smithsonian collection.

Ellen Axson Wilson   This dress, worn by the first Mrs. Woodrow Wilson, is made of white brocaded velvet in a rose design. The narrow hobble skirt is split up the knee over a white satin-and-lace underskirt. The bodice has a net yoke embroidered with rhinestones, steel beads, and pearls. Ellen Wilson died in 1914, a year after her husband became President. The gilt chair has blue-green upholstery; the garlands are gilt.

Grace Goodhue Coolidge   The First Lady wears a dress typical of the "flapper" era, which coincided with the Calvin Coolidge administration (1923–29). It is of red chiffon velvet, featuring a sleeveless bodice, U-neckline, hip-length waistline, and a three-tiered skirt. Matching slippers have rhinestone buckles and gold heels. The gold candelabrum with white candles dates back to the Andrew Jackson administration.

Lou Henry Hoover Typical of the early 1930s, the dress worn by Mrs. Herbert Hoover is made of lustrous pale green satin that falls into bias folds and drapes. Two rhinestone shoulder clips are the only ornamentation. The gold concert grand piano was presented to the United States government by the Steinway company in 1903 for use in the East Room of the White House.

Anna Eleanor Roosevelt   The First Lady wore this gown at the concert that was given (instead of a ball) in honor of Franklin D. Roosevelt's third inauguration in 1941. The color of the satin dress varies from ivory to deep peach, depending on the light. The neckline and sleeves are trimmed with tinted pearls of the same color. The double train widens to several yards at the hem.

Mamie Doud Eisenhower Mrs. Eisenhower was dressed in pink, her favorite color, at Dwight D. Eisenhower's first inaugural ball in 1953. The gown is of pink peau-de-soie with a mauve undertone, and is embroidered with rhinestones. Accessories are of matching pink fabric, including the evening bag, which is silver-framed and encrusted with pink rhinestones, pearls, and beads.

Jacqueline Bouvier Kennedy   The First Lady provided ideas and sketches to the designer for this white silk dress, worn to John F. Kennedy's inaugural ball in 1961. The bodice is embroidered in silver thread, and is veiled overall with white chiffon to give a soft, shimmering effect. The cape is of the same silk, triple-layered with chiffon. An embroidered frog adorns the military collar.

Patricia Ryan Nixon   The First Lady wore this mimosa-yellow silk satin gown with a bolero jacket at the 1969 inaugural ball for Richard M. Nixon. Scrolls of gold and silver bullion are embroidered on the jacket, collar, and cummerbund, which are embellished with crystal jewels. The empire couch is typical of furniture in the White House Red Room as it was refurnished by Mrs. Kennedy.

Rosalynn Smith Carter   The First Lady wore the same gown at Jimmy Carter's inaugural ball in 1977 as she had worn six years earlier at a ball celebrating his inauguration as governor of Georgia. The blue silk chiffon dress is trimmed at waist and wristband with gold braid; the standup collar is covered with gold braid. The fabric of the sleeveless coat is woven with blue-and-gold threads.

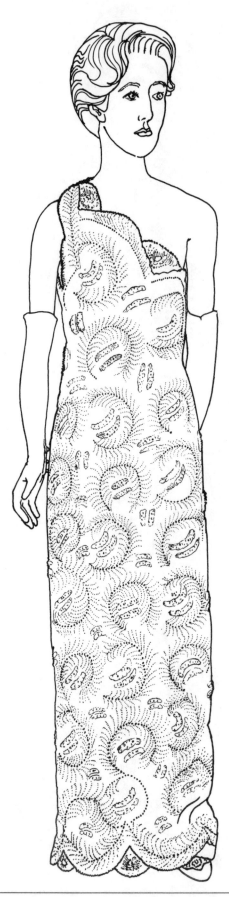

Nancy Davis Reagan This one-shouldered sheath is made of white satin fabric overlaid with lace featuring a fern motif, with the leaves outlined in crystal and chalk beads and the stems of raised bugle beads. Beaded white satin pumps and long white kid gloves complete the ensemble the First Lady wore to eight inaugural balls for Ronald Reagan on January 20, 1981.